MAKING GREAT SALES HAPPEN

Shaping Leaders of Tomorrow

Simple Solutions to Complex Challenges

Kalyankumar S. Hatti

INDIA • SINGAPORE • MALAYSIA

Notion Press

No. 8, 3rd Cross Street
CIT Colony, Mylapore
Chennai, Tamil Nadu – 600004

First Published by Notion Press 2021
Copyright © Kalyankumar S. Hatti 2021
All Rights Reserved.

ISBN
Hardcover: 978-1-64546-525-6
Paperback: 978-1-63832-618-2

This book has been published with all efforts taken to make the material error-free after the consent of the author. However, the author and the publisher do not assume and hereby disclaim any liability to any party for any loss, damage, or disruption caused by errors or omissions, whether such errors or omissions result from negligence, accident, or any other cause.

No part of this book may be used, reproduced in any manner whatsoever without written permission from the author, except in the case of brief quotations embodied in critical articles and reviews.

Dedicated to

This book is dedicated to all the precious people in my life.

My Parents and My Family
Sidram K. Hatti – my father
Boramma K. Hatti – my mother
Jyoti K. Hatti – my wife
Samiksha K. Hatti – my daughter
Sohan K. Hatti – my son

My Teachers
N.M. Bandewar
Padma Iyer

My Mentors
Vinod K. Dasari
R.R.G. Menon
Dr. N. Saravanan
Dr. Venkat Srinivas
T. Venkataraman
Rajinder Singh Sachdeva
V.K. Singh
V.V. Venkataraman
Col. Kaplash
Raju Waghmare
Pathak
Robert Riopel

My Influencers
Shri Sai
Daji Gurav
Yallalinga Prabhu
Sirshree Tejparkhi
Rumina Yasmeen
R. Rajaram

My Coaches
Blair Singer
J. Gabbelini
Christian Mickelsen
Larry
Zoltan
Colton
Sudhir Khot
Monica & Warun
Lynda Gale
Mack Newton
Alex Mandosian
Alan Walter
Dean Graziosi
Tony Robbins
Mahatria

CONTENTS

1. Understanding Your Customer 7
2. Creating Customer Connect. 17
3. Making the Perfect Customer Pitch 23
4. Delivering Customer Profitability. 31
5. Building Customer Realtionships 39
6. Living Customer Relationships. 51
7. Enriching Customer Value 59
8. Ensuring Customer Satisafaction 67

CHAPTER 1

UNDERSTANDING YOUR CUSTOMER

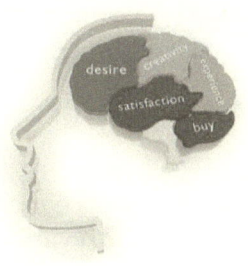

"If you wish to persuade me you must think my thoughts, feel my feelings and speak my words"

– Cicero, Roman Statesman

The customer is the epicentre of any business. Without a customer, there is no business which is why acquiring a customer is very important. To acquire a customer, the first thing we need to do is to understand the customer himself. Without understanding the customer we cannot win over him/her. But how do we understand the customer?

To understand the customer we have to first understand his needs. Every customer has certain expectations from the product or service he is seeking and a salesman who would be able to cater to these expectations. Consumers listen to their guts, the other to the facts, and then a mix of both. They read honest reviews and fake ones. Sometimes they want this, and sometimes that, while what's actually useful for them might be something totally different. Making sense of all that statistics and identifying the customer's true needs and expectations is a tricky task.

Let us understand the basic needs of any consumer.

1) Approachability: The first thing the customer notices is how well he is welcomed when he comes to do business with you. He/she has to be welcomed graciously, sincerely and with warmth. A customer should not feel he/she is intruding on the service provider's work day. He should feel that someone is glad to see him.

2) Understanding and empathy: The customer should feel that the service provider understands why he is here and appreciates his circumstance without criticism or judgement. He should feel that the service provider puts himself in the customer's shoes and understands what is that for which he has come for in the first place. Many customers know what they want or need, but have trouble expressing themselves. This can be because they're not skilled in vocalising their

thoughts, or because they are lost in the terminology of your products or service. In the latter case, consider removing barriers in both areas by implementing a more understandable language.

3) Fairness: All of us want to be treated fairly. The customer should not feel that he is a victim of any class distinction. He should not feel that he has got only the second best and not be left wondering if the 'grass is greener on the other side'. He should not feel annoyed or irritated by the salesman's attitude. They want to know that what they receive is of the highest quality as per the market standard. Consider a study done by a consumer advocate group. They asked samples of airline passengers from numerous airports what they'd paid for their ticket. They found less than 10% of passengers paid the same price for their ticket even though they flew from the same city. The results incited outrage among travellers who saw no justification in paying more, even though they had received the same seating and service.

4) Control: The customer should feel that he has an impact on the events. This need of the customer is to be met with our ability to say "yes" more than we say "no". The rules and policies are not a top priority for the customer. What is important is how reasonably he is treated.

5) Options and alternatives: Customers should feel that there are other options available to him to achieve his goal. They should feel that though they are new to the territory we are there to provide all the inside information and help them in every way we can. It would be pretty upsetting if they feel they have to run around while we knew a better and simpler way all along but never made the suggestion.

6) Information: "Tell me, show me—everything". Customers need to be educated and informed about the products and services thoroughly. They should never feel that the salesman is giving him partial, or worse, false information. They don't want to waste precious time studying about the product or service. They look to us to be their walking, talking, information centre.

Cost and quality: Apart from the six basic needs mentioned above, the customer is always looking for the best deal in terms of cost and quality. He expects to buy something at the lowest cost possible with an assurance of a high quality. This could prove to be a tricky situation for the salesman because to provide a very high-quality product at a low price is not always possible and he has to try to give the customer the best possible option. He has to convince the customer that what he is getting is at the lowest cost and of the best quality.

A company's after-sales service and the support information that is provided to the customer after he has bought the product, is extremely important. After sales service makes sure products and services meet or surpass the expectations of the customer. It ensures customer satisfaction and customer retention. It generates loyal customers. When a customer is looking for a product, he is also looking at the after-sales service record of the company.

Once the basic need of the customer is understood, we then have to understand the mentality or the mind-set of the customer. Every day we come across different types of customers and each has to be dealt with differently. These customers and their mind-sets can be broadly classified into four categories. Let us study each one of them in some detail.

1) The Director: The name itself suggests that we are dealing with a very demanding customer. He is the take- charge type of customer. He wants what he wants and when he wants it. He is not into small talks and wants all the facts in one go so that he can take a rapid decision. He wants the product at the lowest price possible and has to be delivered when he wants it and that is usually immediately. Such a customer has to be dealt with carefully. He has to be

complimented and presented with facts to the point. Do not deviate from the subject and do not confront him anyway. Don't get lured into any discussion and discuss things calmly and professionally. Stay confident and point out the good quality and performance of the product.

2) The Analytical Customer: This type includes customers who research and analyse all the possibilities before making a decision. They require accuracy and analysis. They want data, facts and details. Analyticals read manuals, directions and the fine print. The advantage here is that they have done their homework and comparisons and researched the product well. Such customers are all about facts and data. If the product has detailed labelling, give it to them. They are a good source of information and may sometimes know more than the owner or the salesman. Their decision to purchase is many a time based on how the product reflects their social status.

3) The Relater type: The Relater personality type of customer has a strong need to feel part of a group. They prefer to keep everyone on their network and refer to them as 'my'. They always know someone who knows someone who knows someone. The easiest way to sell a product to them is to simply ask them. The bottom line is to include them in any possible way

you can. They are wonderful customers and a never-ending source of referrals.

4) The Socialiser: They are customers who love to talk, are outgoing and love to make new friends. They want to build a relationship with the people who work in the store. If they don't like you they won't do business with you. They want to build friendships. If they can build friendships in different stores, they will go to different stores. They like to give and receive compliments. If you give them fact and figures they will shut down. However, they are self-centred. They would like to go to a store where they are made to feel important. The best way to deal with them is to use compliments liberally.

Remember their names and make their shopping experience as much fun and entertaining as possible.

Apart from these four types of customers, there are several other types which can become a guideline for you to deal with them when you come across these types of customers. I will briefly touch upon some more types of customers.

The Silent type: The most difficult type of customer to deal with is the one who is not ready does not utter a single word. Dealing with such a customer is often monotonous and fearsome. It is very difficult to know what is going on in the mind of such a customer and hence it becomes difficult to give him options or suggestions. There are two ways to deal with such a customer. One is to take his silence as consent and proceed with the sale. The second would be to ask him questions like," Don't you agree with this Sir?" or ask him. "Sir, what is your opinion on this?" A persistent friendliness on the part of the salesman would bring satisfactory results.

The Impulsive type: These types of customers do not have any particular product in mind. They usually tend to buy something that catches their attention. It is difficult to handle such customers as they don't know what they want and they expect the salesman to display all the useful products. Such a customer should be allowed to go through various products before they can decide. If treated properly this kind of customer can increase the percentage of sales. The salesman should find out the reason as to why the particular customer is hesitating and has not come to a final decision. After finding out the reason he should give sufficient information besides logically explaining why the customer should purchase and then give him time to make his decision.

The Impatient type: Such customers want to be attended to immediately and may get angry or irritated if things don't go their way. Some are so impatient that they may even leave the shop if not attended to immediately.

The salesman here should not waste time and attend to the customer on a priority basis. He should not waste time in looking for goods as this may irritate the customer. The greatest advantage in dealing with such a customer is that they will not bargain with you as they think that bargaining is a waste of time.

Need-based Customer: These customers have a very specific thing or product in mind that they wish to buy. They may also have a specific need for a particular product. For example, a suit for an event. These customers are frequent but don't always result in sales. Show this customer what you can do to satisfy their need. Most of the time it is difficult to satisfy such customers. These customers must be handled positively and given good reasons to buy an alternate product. They have to be convinced that what they have in mind and what they are buying is the same thing. They should be reasoned with that the product they are buying will definitely satisfy their need. But don't rush them through the interaction because by doing so you may lose the customer.

Loyal Customer: These customers are very few but generally promote the sales and help in increasing the profits. These customers come back to you again and again as they are very satisfied with your product. Therefore it is very important to deal with them very carefully. Be in touch with them on a regular basis and invest more time and effort with them. Loyal customers need individual attention and demand respect and politeness. They will use a particular business for the experience that they have had. Sometimes cost does not play a role here. They are ready to pay a little extra to get the product they want.

As a salesman, your focus should be to bring in more and more loyal customers into your fold. You should expand the range of products to cater to the other impulsive customers and strategize your sales talk depending on the type of customer you are encountering. Your aim should be to provide a good experience to the customer thereby converting an impulsive customer into a loyal one.

Next time a customer walks into your store size him/her up and put them into one of these personality categories. You will then be better prepared to interact with each customer on a higher level and increase your sales drastically.

CHAPTER 2

CREATING CUSTOMER CONNECT

"Your Customer doesn't care how much you know until they know how much you care"
– Damon Richards

In the previous chapter, we learnt about the mind-set of the customer which plays an important part in how we can connect with the customer. It helps in strategizing the methods we use to connect with the customer.

The question that can arise here is how important is this connect with the customer?

Yes, it is very important to connect with the customer. But what is more important is to connect with the customer in the right way.

Let me give you an example here. You switch on your laptop, work hard on preparing all the data, reports and then send it to the customer. But in all this, you forget to put on your Wi-Fi or the LAN connection. Though the reports are ready and you have mailed it, it does not reach the destination as there is no Wi-Fi or LAN connection. Unless the connection is on, your mail doesn't reach the intended customer. Without the connection, the communication is only with yourself and not the customer.

The next question that arises is how do we connect with the customer?

The best skill here is 'observation'. One has to keep his eyes open to see the things that others might miss. You have to observe your customer very carefully. His body language can tell you a lot of things about him and his intentions and also his mind-set. You have to keep your ears open to hear what he says. Then you have to have an open heart to receive what you are not hearing. In fact, shift to a conscious mental state. You can start the conversation based on what is in the customer's mind. This is like a radar scan. If you listen to the customer carefully he may utter something that will give a hint of what he wants. It could be a challenge he is facing with his business or something to do with a particular service or product. One has to be attentive to find his problem and then give him solutions to fix it. But be very cautious here. A problem is a problem only if the customer recognises it. If we think it's a problem but the customer is not finding the situation or a task a problem then we should not try to fix it. This is like pouring water into a pot which is upside down. The pot will never be filled. This means you will never sell anything to the customer. We acknowledge and fix a problem from the customer's point of view.

It is essential to know what the customer needs and the needs are met with if you want a long-term relationship with the customer. Most customers do not have the clarity of what they want and are unable to express this need to the service reps. You simply require more information to know what's best for them. These questions will help:

"What would you like the product to do for you?"

First of all, ask the customer what product he is looking for and what its use would be for him. The customer needs the product for a specific reason or a general use. Once this need or want of the customer is understood you can show him a product or products that would meet his need. Also keep in mind that the customer could be looking for something new, a new trend or the look of the product. In such a case show him the latest product in the market that would meet his need.

"What is the issue you want to solve?"

Ask this question to the customer to know what he specifically wants. This question will give you an idea of what the customer's problem or issue is and how you can help him to solve it. The ability to fix the issue is the product's benefit and that is what the customer is actually looking for.

"How much are you willing to spend?"

Money is a matter of concern to nearly every customer you will encounter. But he may not be able to understand whether the product/service he is paying is worth it or not. He may not be able to understand the value of the product in terms of the benefit he is going to get and the price he is paying for that. So as a salesman you have to give the customer a comparable table of cost and benefits so that he gets an idea of what he is getting for the money he is willing to spend.

Once you understand what the customer wants then you can suggest solutions and meet his needs. You can talk about how another customer had faced a similar situation and how it was solved, what role you or your company played in the solving the problem. Thereby the customer was happy and you contributed constantly to his business and his profits.

When you do the above you are actually prequalifying yourself and your company as an authoritative and reliable source, in helping the customers. In the process you are building the trust and making the connection with the customer, moving from a weak Wi-Fi connection to a strong one.

All we talked so far was of pre-sales, starting from nowhere to identifying a signal, checking if that is the right hot-spot. Analysing if that is the right problem if it is that the right challenge. Then we check if it is right from your perspective, is it right from the customer's perspective and then qualifying yourself and your company and ensuring that you have built the bridge across to the customer.

CHAPTER 3

MAKING THE PERFECT CUSTOMER PITCH

"It's not the employer who pays the wages. Employers only handles the money. It's the customer who pays the wages."
– Henry Ford

In the last chapter, we built the bridge that reaches the customer. We have connected with the customer. Now you have to decide what best suits the customer's needs. Which service that we provide will make him happy. The solution to the problem should satisfy the customer.

The solution or the product that is being provided to the customer can't be given away all at once. It has to be introduced slowly to the customer. Introduce the solution or a product in instalments and not all at once. This would help you assess the reaction of the customer to your views and if there is a change required, you can make them accordingly before presenting it to the customer. Some product or service requires more than a great introduction to attract the customer. Your presentation should offer a summary of key points, respond to questions and queries, explain benefits and provide facts that will help the person decide whether to become your business's customer.

For example, if a customer wants to fly from Delhi to Bangalore and if he logs into your travel portal you have to provide comparative prices of different airlines, the different flights that are available, the lowest prices and most importantly, why should the customer book his tickets through your portal. You have to give some incentive or gifts that will attract the customer to your company. You can hold back some information until the time the customer is confirming his booking. It is like showing the trailer for a movie to the viewer. Instead of giving away the whole thing introduce the product gradually. You have to build the curiosity and expectation of the customer.

The product is the hero or the main character of the movie. The product has to talk for itself. You have to show the customer that your product is unique and better equipped to meet the needs of the customer. All the advertising expense in the world won't help a bad product, and you need to be confident that your product delivers on its brand promise. You know what that is — it's what you tell your customers your product is going to do for them. Does it deliver on the brand promise consistently?

Before you design your product you have to take the customer's feedback into consideration. David Ciccaralli says, "My favourite one-question survey I've participated in was, "What can we do that will knock your socks off?" Present it as one question and one large text box for your customers to answer in. Try it. I promise that you'll learn a lot."

You have to pay attention to one more thing here. If you hold a major share of the market then you have to keep more than one product at hand with a slight variation. The wider the range of products the greater is the curiosity of the customer to check out your products. They feel they have more choices with you and also get better value for their money as there are different variants. If you are a significant market player you will not have say Product A and Product B. But you will have variants of the same product i.e., you will have A1, A2, A3, A4 etc., and similarly B1, B2, B3, B4 etc.

For example, the car manufacturer Maruthi Suzuki offered you different versions of the same car say 'Swift'.

This car comes in petrol and diesel versions. Further, you have different variants in Swift giving you choice to choose from different variants according to your budget and also your requirement. But here is the catch i.e., you have to be careful when you are displaying the products to the customer. When you are sharing the variants of the products A or B, first of all, see to it that it makes sense to the customer. You have given comparisons of the products highlighting their differences and what makes each of the products unique and how each can benefit the customer. You have to keep your eyes open for his non-verbal gestures, his facial expressions, and his body language. These will tell you a lot about what the customer is thinking of your product and accordingly, you can make the changes suitable to the customer's needs. You can then fix the variant most suitable to the need of the customer for which you get the positive gesture from the customer. It all depends on your observation.

For example when you are talking about one product, though the customer is listening to you he is looking somewhere else. He is listening but his eyes are focused on something else. His facial expression will tell you whether he is interested in the product or not. If he is really interested in the product his stance will tell you. He will pay you full attention. You as a salesman should read between the lines and understand whether the customer is interested in your product or not.

Another example could be that of a child who has come to buy a doll. A doll on the shelf has caught the child's attention. The salesman is showing the child and parents different dolls and talking about each one's uniqueness. But the child is not interested in all this talk. His mind is set on that particular doll and wants to buy only that even though his parents feel that it is not appropriate or for the same price he may get a better one. But the child does not understand this logic. He has liked the doll and he wants that particular doll only. Then as a salesman, it is your knack to convince the parents to buy that doll itself for the child. So, folks, a lot of your sales depend on your observation of your customer's behaviour.

Now you have your fish in the net. You can now start sharing the value of your product, USP details, and benefits of each product, its uniqueness and also the differences between the products. You have to convince the customer as to why he should buy your product and not some other. This can be done by showing how unique your product or service is and how the customer will benefit the most if he buys this particular product. All this should make sense to the customer. Be cautious as there may be pressure to sell it. But do not let the cat out. You have to give a value proposition. The price is always held on until the end. The most common mistake is to give away the price. This will switch off the customer no matter how much value you add to your product. Whatever else you say starts appearing to the customer's mind as 'cost, cost, and cost'.

Once you are done with the value proposition and its advantages to the customer and his business show him/her a couple of testimonials. What are you doing by showing testimonials? You are giving proofs. This is where things get a little sensitive when we are talking about a customer's belief. Is this the product or service the customer wants to buy from you?

What is a testimonial? Testimonials are the supports which increase your credibility and level of expertise. They are the proof of faith that people have in you and your company. It is an important tool to attract a prospective customer, create a deeper interest in your customers and ultimately make you and your business become increasingly successful. The success of a business depends heavily on word of mouth. Testimonials are extremely powerful tools in strengthening your branding. People will not do business with you if they don't trust you and find that you are not credible. This is the best way to show your potential customers the faith that the earlier customers place in you and also shows how trustworthy you are. As the word passes from one person to another slowly your business also goes on the upward curve.

The testimonials have to be used effectively to help your business. Testimonials are not only about selling your products and/or services. They are also about your successful, positive interactions with other people. They are the embodiment of the relationship that you share with those people. Share your testimonial with as many people as you can and in as many places as possible. They serve two purposes. First, it will strengthen your reputation and presence in the market and secondly, it will serve as a thank you to the person who took so much trouble to write it for you.

Credibility is essential to the success of your business. Strategic and intelligent use of testimonials can go a long way in promoting your business. The more online visibility and stronger reputation you have and continue to maintain, the stronger your business will become.

Now comes the part where the cat has to be let out: the price. To summarise, by tagging the price with the top two or three key benefits, it's the bell in the cat's neck. Always keep a cushion on the price you share with the customer. You should price the product in such a way that if required you should be able to bring down the price without hurting your profits. You should earn a healthy profit but try not to be too greedy. If you have priced your product too high then it will be difficult. But pricing it too low and then bringing it further down will also hurt your business. Try to maintain a middle ground.

One more thing, don't cut the price too low as then the customer will start wondering how much profit you are making. Quote a decent price and stick to it.

One important thing here is the closure. The customer has to have the feeling that he has got what he had asked for in terms of the value. You have to show that he/she has got what he/she wanted. He should feel that he is getting his money's worth.

CHAPTER 4

DELIVERING CUSTOMER PROFITABILITY

"The ones who are crazy enough to think that they can change the world are the ones who do."

— *Steve Jobs*

Welcome to the world of money! It is the world of profit, the world of positive flow which every businessman expects. In the last chapter, we saw the salesman getting ready to make the sale. But actually, the sale has just begun.

How do you call a sale successful? Is it when you have collected the advance for the product but are yet to deliver the product or is it when you invoice the product or is it when you deliver the product or when you receive the due from the bank?

The true sale is when the service or the product you have sold starts working for the owner and starts churning results for the customer. The product has to add value to the customer by not only generating income but it should be a prized possession for the customer. This is called value-added selling. In today's marketplace where so many products or services are viewed as a commodity, the ability to add value through your product or service is an absolute necessity. But here you should know the customer's definition of value and not your own. You have to play according to the need of the customer and his concept of value.

In short, it starts when the product you have sold adds value to the customer's business and moreover it should add value without any trouble. Imagine you went to a restaurant to enjoy dinner with your family. The food was really good. But what a customer remembers along with the quality of food is the quality of service. How was this tasty food served? How quick or how slow was the service? Was the food hot? Sometimes when you order all the courses at once it really depends on the hotel management to see that the food served is at the right pace. First, the starter is served then the main course and then the dessert. When you have ordered the food you expect the food to come one after the other. If the food is brought all at once you will not enjoy the dinner. Or say the service at the restaurant is really slow and every time you order something and the waiter has not got the water or served the roti or delayed bringing a side dish, served the rice but delayed the dal. Or if everything went well but you are made to wait for the bill for half an hour, then how would you rate your experience in this restaurant? You would say the food was great, but you add a 'but' to your sentence and explain your displeasure or unhappiness. You are not feeling great about the experience.

Now the question that arises here is would you go back to this same place after this experience or would you recommend it to your friends. No, never! So this is like credit but immediately debited. The experience doesn't remain with the customer. Hence, folks, the sale is not yet done.

The next step after you close the sale is to walk along with the customer to give him a delightful experience of being with you, with your company, with your brand, a brand that he would cherish, a brand that he would look forward to continue working with. Let us say you have given a wonderful experience to the customer in all that is mentioned above.

In his book, My Life in Advertising, advertising pioneer Claude Hopkins tells the story of how in the

1920's he used a new advertising campaign to propel Schlitz beer from fifth place in the beer market to being tied for first.

After being hired for the job, Hopkins toured the brewery to get to know the product. He discovered an elaborate filtration process in which the beer was sterilized and cooled in a special way over frigid pipes - all in a plate glass room in which only filtered air could enter. When he asked why they weren't telling people about this he was told that 'every brewery filtered beer this way'.

His response? "But others have never told this story." Schlitz rolled out their new 'filtration story' and marched forward to beer brand dominance.

The next step in the journey is to have the machine or product or service add value. But how do you define value? What are your products or services actually worth to the customers? Value is an important tactic that can be used by small businesses to acquire and retain customers.

The art of creating value starts with the ability to see your business through the eyes of the customer. The business may lose out if we focus on features instead of benefits. You have to shift your focus from providing content to the needs of the customer then you can start helping and stop selling. People don't pay for the product or services. They pay for what these products or services can do for them. Only when you create something 'significant' for others and focus on the customer, the customer will buy whatever you are selling. The customer should feel that he is buying much more worth than the money he is paying. The customer is ready to pay more if he feels he is getting 'more' for his money. This 'more' is what creates the value of the product or service you are providing. His satisfaction is an important benchmark in adding value to your product or service.

Once the customer feels that your product or service is really valuable he will not only come back to you but will also recommend your company to family and friends. By adding value you are not only retaining your earlier customer you are also creating new customers for your business, thereby expanding your customer base and hence your brand value, brand name and profitability.

Let us come to the value that the product or service is adding to the customer's business. In other words, the product is giving the money back to the owner. In this working model, the customer needs to enjoy a delightful experience just like the example we discussed. In short, the product or service should be trouble free, reliable and delivered on time. Only then the transaction means credit, then to the owner's bank and the customer feels proud and free of hassles to enjoy the benefits or profitability of his business.

The crux of this attribute of profitability from the business perspective is to ensure that the product is reliable, trouble-free, operational experience is delightful and in case of abnormality the customer is attended to immediately and is insulated from any kind of bad or undesired experience of the product or service. The bottom line remains intact that the product should perform well so that the customer remains in your net.

For example, a few years ago, Coca-Cola started selling the 8-ounce mini-cans. They anticipated a consumer trend towards counting calories and becoming more health conscious.

Per ounce, the mini-can isn't cheaper than the regular can. In some cases, the price could even be the same as the regular 12 ounce can.

So why would someone pay the same amount for less? Don't we all want a deal?

Coke did its homework and found that the mini-cans reduced the amount of guilt that a consumer felt for snacking while minimizing the chances of overeating.

Coke realized that consumers were no longer relying on the value-for-money as the sole factor in deciding to buy.

Instead, consumers wanted to eat smaller portions, particularly in the sub-100 calories area which Kraft originally started with its mini snack packs of chips, cookies and crackers.

The company understood the emotional needs of their customers and they provided a solution to solve their problem without losing their brand integrity or customer perceived value. The product is still the same, just smaller portions.

CHAPTER 5

BUILDING CUSTOMER REALTIONSHIPS

"The customer's perspective is your reality."
– *Kate Zabriskie*

In the last chapter, we learnt the elements of a sale for a customer from the profitability perspective. In short, one needs to save on the assets side, making sure the customer doesn't put you or your company on the liability side of the business: the gain, the customer can write off anytime.

Assuming the positive side of the sale is not over yet. Yes, from the transaction point of view the sale is over. But from the company perspective and long-term vision, the sale is not over yet. We are now on the sale journey.

The next step is to nurture the relationship that has been built by the product between the customer and your product and your company. It's all about finding people who believe in your product or service. Powerful relationships don't happen with one time meetings or from a business card. Once a relationship is established it has to be followed up on. You have to be in constant touch with the customer and take his feedback. You have to ensure the growth of the relationship. You have to slowly build a network which will turn your contacts into customers. Networking is a long-term investment. Communicate like you business's life depends on it. Build your reputation as an expert by giving some free advice. An easy way to do this is by sending short emails to the potential customers giving them tips, or telling them more about your product. If they like what they read they will definitely forward it to others and this is like introducing you through word of mouth. Once you have done the networking and also followed up, then be sure that the customer will come back to you again and also bring with him, new customers. Business is all about relationships. Find them, nurture them and let your sales soar. Let us understand the relationship first.

In the modern world, we have heard of so many relationships dying and we have also heard of so many relationships built on strong values and principles. "Without strong relationships, it is impossible to have success as a business owner," says Michael Denisoff, who is the founder and CEO of Denisoff Consulting Group, California. He says this was a lesson he had to learn the hard way when, a while ago, he fell into the trap of neglecting some of his business relationships. The first instance was when he called up a supplier to ask for a favor–not realizing how much time had gone by from the last time he had touched base.

Denisoff says, his supplier seemed distant and not very willing to help him out, which was surprising. After asking him if anything was wrong, Denisoff's supplier answered that since Denisoff hadn't been around for a while, he felt like he was being taken advantage of. In another instance, he called up a customer who he could tell was not pleased with him because, in truth, he only called her when she had a project ready to go. She felt like Denisoff did not truly value her and was using her only for her business. It's like having a friend that only comes to see you when they want to borrow money or need help moving, he says. "In time, you cut them off."

The evident relationships in the world are a two-way connection. Similarly, in a completed sale or a delivered product, forgetting the customer will make it a one-way relationship - an unsustainable relationship. What we need here is a two-way relationship, a two-way response and behaviour, a two-way experience that both parties respect, that which both the partners enjoy and resonate with, that which both parties value and would like to continue. It has to be a relationship where small misunderstandings don't affect your business; a relationship where there is a lot of scope for communication and that communication is always two ways i.e., the customer and the salesman are able to speak to each other quite openly.

The most important factor in a relationship is trust. The customer has to trust that the company will deliver its promises and the company trusts that the customer will be loyal to the company. This trust slowly builds a confidence in both the parties that the sale is going in the right direction and they can depend on each other and this relationship is going to be a long-term one. In short, it is 'bharose ki baat'.

After saying all this you may ask what has all this to do with customer relationship. Yes, it has a lot to do. It tells us how to build a relationship between the salesman, the customer and the company.

Everything depends on how the company responds to the customer- a response not based on action, a response not based on an event but a response to the event. However, happy a company keeps its customer there is bound to be a complaint once in a while. Even if the customer doesn't sound as if he is complaining he is definitely bringing something to your attention that needs an immediate response. The speed of the response can decide whether the customer will return to you or not. If your response is too slow the customer may feel neglected and decide to go somewhere else for his requirements. This way the company will lose a valuable customer. This should be avoided at all costs.

"Service recovery from failures" (when the organization fails to meet customer expectations) should always be immediate, explains Taryn Brown, PhD., who has more than 15 years of experience in working in customer service for companies such as Walt Disney World and The Daytona International Speedway, and is an assistant professor of hospitality management at Daytona State

College. "The goal of all employees of an organization should be on-the-spot recovery."

As she explains, it is a complex issue, because customers don't want to wait and may become even more agitated by having to do so. Yet employees working with customers may lack the power to efficiently handle the situation, which may lead to a delay in the problem being addressed.

All this depends on how you have built the relationship with the customer. It's like saying I will live on the first floor of a house. This is possible only if the first floor is built, otherwise, it's only an illusion. You will enjoy the experience only after you have built it.

While waiting for take-off in Tampa, Florida, Peter Shankman jokingly asked Morton's Steakhouse to deliver a porterhouse steak when he landed at Newark airport. While departing the Newark airport to meet his driver, he was greeted by Morton's server with a 24 oz. Porterhouse steak, shrimp, potatoes, and bread – the works. A full meal and no bill.

When you think of the logistics of pulling this off, it becomes even more impressive. The Community Manager needed to get approval and place the order. It needed to be prepared and then driven by the server to the airport, to the correct location and at the right time. All in less than three hours.

Some of the comments on Peter's post suggest that this isn't an anomaly. Another reader shares his experience of ordering a baked potato and getting a full steak meal – delivered and for free.

Takeaway: Do something unexpected for a loyal customer – when they want it most and least expect it.

Now let's get to the core of this matter. It takes only a fraction of a second to break a relationship but it takes considerable hard work and dedication to build a customer relationship. To understand this more clearly, let's say you met with an accident in the middle of a highway and you are badly in need of help. A stranger stops by to help you. This help by the stranger is very crucial at this point in time as it has helped save your life. He makes you feel great and valuable. Your faith in humanity is restored as you were thinking you may not get any help and certainly not from a stranger. He is with you when you needed him the most. What has the stranger done here? He has built a relationship with a helping hand and you reciprocate it by showing gratitude towards him. Would you not remember this stranger and experience throughout your life? Yes, you will! You feel very grateful to this stranger, value his memory. If you come across any situation you will remember the stranger and how he helped you. Whether you meet him again or not you will always remember his timely help. So the context of the business here is to keep your tower charged to catch any signal or any event when the customer is in trouble or feels helpless in relation to the product that he has bought. In such an event the company rushes to his help with its resources to restore the product's service. Let's take a more optimistic view, say, the product is working fine, everything is going hunky dory and let's hope there are no adversities.

The company has to keep its radar fine-tuned to catch the signal and also understand what the signal means. The company has to be alert to any complaints or requests by the customer. You cannot ignore it however small it may seem. Moreover, this relationship is a long-term one. You can't stop responding today and then think that when you contact your customer after a long time he will respond to you with the same zest that he had done earlier. Let me give you an example. Parents give birth to children and everything is fine. They are quite a distance apart yet share a good relationship with each other. After 20 years the father needs the son/daughter as in a typical Indian movie, will the child say "Hello Papa" with the same energy and bonding they shared earlier? No, it does not work that way. It will happen only when the relationship is built further, made stronger, woven tighter and valued more. Otherwise, it's just a biological parent-child relationship. It becomes a bulb without light. Both the parties have to make an effort to keep the relationship alive and this has to be done constantly. It is not a one-day affair. It's for lifetime and effort has to be put every day. Similarly, the company has to be in touch with the loyal customers constantly and be ready to go that extra step to satisfy the customer.

The core here is regarding customer relationship. It is all about how the relation is built, how this connection is taken forward. Make sure that you are around the customer. This need not be physically but see to it that you are available on a call when he needs you and you respond genuinely as soon as possible. Remember how hard life is. We go to a doctor only when we are ill. When we go to the clinic or hospital we expect the doctor to take care of us immediately. We expect the doctor to be available hands-on and relieve us of our pain and stress.

When we are given immediate attention and treatment we feel good and would like to come back to the same doctor if something happens again. But this is only one part of the working relationship? What if the doctor keeps in touch with you even when you are healthy, keeps an eye on you, reminds you about your annual health check-up or critical preventive check-up etc.? How would this kind of a relationship be? This would definitely be a happy and enjoyable experience. Similarly, if you keep in touch with your customer even when he does not require anything, but just to remind him that you are there for his needs then he would feel great and important. The next time a need arises within his circle of family or friends, he would remember you. This is exactly the way the company needs to make the customer feel. What do you feel when the customer calls you saying he needs another one of your products or recommend you to his friend or his business colleague who also needs to buy the same product? Surely, it is you and your company which will receive the call. Then you can proudly say that I and my company have built that relationship.

How is this kind of rapport built between the customer and the company? For this, you have put in a little more effort. You have to improve the way your customers experience your service. Like I said earlier the response time is very important. You have to acknowledge that you have received the customer's request or complaint and will take further action. This can be done in many ways. For example, you can send an email stating that you have received the customer's email and will look into the matter. You can call up and tell them that their request is being processed. Further, you can inform the customer of the progress that is taking place concerning his work. When you are constantly in touch with the customer and keep him in the loop with what's happening he will definitely feel important and also that he is being taken seriously and is given his due credit.

The old adage "Customer is king" may be clichéd but it is true now and forever.

Do you know 55% of customers are ready to pay high for guaranteed good customer experience? Also, 67% would churn if they encounter a bad experience with a company. Your customers are the reason you exist or grow and any misstep here can drown you forever. No wonder, the pundits always zero on ensuring good customer relationships. That is why once you build the relationship with customer nurture it, grow it and only then will you and your company will be successful.

CHAPTER 6

LIVING CUSTOMER RELATIONSHIPS

"There is extraordinary chemistry that exists in long-term relationships"
– *Conrad Levinson*

Relationship. What is a relationship? A relationship is a key to your life. What does a relationship do in your life? It could be a relationship with yourself, your family, your relatives, your friends, with nature, animals etc. In this chapter, we will learn how we need to manage the customer relationship and sustain the same.

We will start with the fact that you have made the sale; you have begun a new relationship with the customer. The first question that comes to your mind is when you have already made the sale does the relationship matter? Let us understand this with an example.

It's a Sunday morning, and you are out for a walk. You see a stray dog following you and you feel that you should give it some food. You decide to offer it a piece of bread. So you purchase a piece of bread and feed it. You feel good about it and go about your work. The next day, at the same time you notice another dog and repeat the same. This continues for a week. You have started something new in your life which makes you feel good about yourself. The point to be noted here is that each day it was a different dog. All of this was the start of a new relationship. If you want the relationship to continue you have to make an effort every day. If you fed the dog one day and not the next day, you cannot expect the dog to come to you when he sees you. New relationships can be held on to only with constant effort and repeated meetings. This analogy can be applied to human beings. You could introduce yourself to a new person every day; give him/her your card throughout the week. It is not enough if you just give the card and expect the customer to come running to you. You have to find out customer's need and see that you provide the best product or service. Only then will this relationship continue.

Now pause for a minute. If you observe closely, you realize that you are still strangers whether it is the dog or a human being. It is like seeding the tree and expecting the tree to grow. No, that doesn't work as per the law of the universe. Everything needs nurturing, care and bonding to bring out the results. The tree needs to be nurtured with water, not randomly but consistently. The quality is secondary, consistency comes first. No matter how small the quantity of water, if nurtured consistently you will one day see the seed grow into a plant and eventually into a tree. Now when the tree is grown it will offer you shelter irrespective of whether you are watering it any longer or not. This is true of human beings also. You have to exchange, discuss, nurture, build a bond slowly and consistently and find some means of growing the relationship. Then you have the best friend. Once you nurture and become friends then you can and will pull each other, push each other, acknowledge each other and respect each other. That's a relationship – whether in a personal space or a business place.

Consistency is important, especially in business. You may have heard the saying: If you are persistent, you get it and if you are consistent, you keep it. Being consistent is the difference between success and failure. Consistency is a must as you build and grow your business. Leadership guru John Maxwell said: "Small disciplines repeated with consistency every day lead to great achievements, gained slowly over time."

Restaurants, for example, must be consistent, because customers come in expecting the same good food all the time. If they slip up even one day, they lose customers. Consistency establishes reputations. When people get what they want, they are happy and they come back. Customers expect the same standards.

Until you have tried something new for a period of time and in a consistent manner, you cannot decide if it works or not. How do you measure effectiveness if what you are measuring isn't performed consistently?

As a manager or a team leader, you have to be consistent in your attitude and behaviour. This will set an example for your employees and build trust in your customers. Also, your customers and your employees need a predictable flow of information from you. You have to constantly be in touch with your customers and this consistent connection makes a difference of success in business.

This is the kind of relationship we are talking about with the customers. How do we turn an ordinary customer into an extraordinary customer? The answer lies in the relationship. When it comes to business relationships it is about your consideration about the customer's win. Whatever product or service you provide to the customer has to be beneficial to him. The customer will do business with you only when he knows that your first priority is his benefit and not the company's profit. Only when the customer is benefitted will the company's business and profit grow. Customer's satisfaction decides whether he will continue to do business with you or not. It provides a metric which can be used to measure and improve business performance. It will also tell you about the loyalty of the customer. With cut-throat competition in the market, you have to constantly strive to create an environment of complete customer satisfaction. Customer service plays a major role in retaining the old and loyal customers and also in bringing new ones.

Are you adding value to his business as you win? Remember that as time goes usage loses its importance and value. The relationship loses its value and importance and also the value of your product. This is assuming that the basic relationship is in place because if the basic relationship of trust, mutual respect, manner, gestures, commands and confidence is not in place then it is like disconnecting on you LAN and expecting that your mail has reached the destination. The mail only appears to have been sent but actually, it is lying in your outbox.

The context here is of serving the customer and his business through your product or service. Once the sale is done it does not stop there. You have to follow it up with after sales service. This after-sales service makes all the difference to your business. Customer service is often the only contact that the customer has with the company. Some customers spend thousands and even lakhs of rupees per year with a company. Consequently, when they have a question or product issue, they expect a company's customer service department to resolve their issues. A company with excellent customer service is more likely to get repeat business from customers.

Consequently, the company will benefit with greater sales and profits. Contrarily, companies with poor customer service may lose customers, which will have a negative impact on business. It costs a lot more money for a company to acquire a customer than to retain them, due to advertising costs and the expense of sales calls. Therefore, the efforts that go into maintaining quality customer service can really pay dividends over time. People with a positive experience with your company will tell their family and friends about this and encourage new customers to come to you. This will be positive publicity for your company. Always go beyond the sales or else it becomes a messy transaction. Ability to stand by your product or service, incorporating critical feedbacks or changes that are required, offering after sales service, listening to the issues, continuous improvement of the product make your sales more and more efficient. You also become more productive, competent and stay relevant in the market. All this will get you into a sound and stable customer relationship.

Dedication is what will lead you and your company to great heights. It is repeat sales, references, word of mouth which add to your business. All this means increased sales, increased numbers and increased profits. You have to be dedicated to the business you're trying to build and the goals you're trying to achieve. Without dedication, little else will matter. You have to stay focused on your goal. When your dedication is to help others when you put your customers first: success will definitely be yours. Dedication is a major factor in making your business successful. Without customers, you won't have a business to be dedicated to. Whenever I need a reminder of how important dedication is to reaching your goals I think of Victor Hugo.

He started writing Les Miserables in the 1830s and it took him 17 years to finish it.

I can only imagine his level of dedication. To start a project that would take almost two decades to complete seems almost incomprehensible to me.

Yet his dedication paid off. His book has been considered one of the greatest novels of the nineteenth century.

The other side of the coin is also true and you have to be prepared for a one-time credit and debit too. Both sides have to take this into consideration.

CHAPTER 7

ENRICHING CUSTOMER VALUE

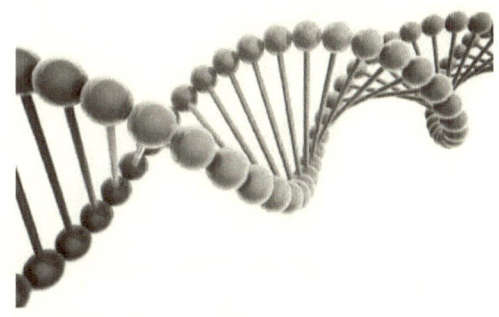

"Your Customers dream of a happier and better life. Don't move products. Instead enrich lives."
- Steve Jobs

Welcome to the world of value: That world for which the customers pay and hope that they get more value than the cost of the product or service. In this chapter let us understand the importance of value to the customer and also clarify the confusion of cost versus value.

There is always this confusion in the customer's mind regarding the value and cost of a product. When a customer asks, 'What does this cost?' he is actually not only asking in terms of money but also the intrinsic value of the product. When the seller tells it costs 'x', he then relates it to the benefit, usage, the profit, the leverage etc. and internally debates whether it is worth buying this particular product or service. Now apart from owning the product the customer should also feel some emotional satisfaction in buying it. This is where the value of the product comes into play.

Let us understand this through an example. You have decided to buy an elephant for yourself or your daughter. You go to a shop, look at several elephants; one in the centre of the showroom attracts you and you ask the shopkeeper to show it to you and ask, "How much does this cost?" The salesman answers ₹ 500. You then ask the cost of the adjacent one and the answer is ₹ 300. You then ask the cost of another one and the answer is ₹ 100. You now stop for a while and think which one of these elephants you should buy. Perhaps you end up buying the elephant that costs ₹ 100 or the one that costs ₹ 300 based on your budget.

Now consider the same situation in another shop which has the same models of elephants. When you enter the shop, a salesman accompanies you and says, "Good

Morning Sir. How can I help you? Please tell me what you are looking for, so that I can guide you."

In the second situation the first deposit is done by the salesman in your mind. You answer, "I am looking for an elephant toy." The salesman replies, "Great Sir. We have one of the best collections of toys in the city ranging from Rs.50 to Rs.5000. May I know your budget Sir, so that I can offer you the best." Appreciating the enthusiasm of the salesman you reply, "Around 300 to 500". Based on this interaction, he goes on to show you various elephants saying, "Here is the budget elephant; here is the premium elephant and ultra-premium elephant etc." Before the customer looks with a confused state of mind, the salesman says he is the caretaker of the elephants and will explain everything about the elephants. This will help you make the right choice and an informed decision and the child will love it. Yes, the salesman here has created another emotional deposit.

The conversation goes on. The salesman gives you the details of how the particular elephant is made up of child friendly material, how its eyes are painted with long lasting paint, his trunk is movable, the ears can also be moved. The tail of the elephant comes with a patented technology and can rotate 360 degrees. He further says,

"I am sure your child will carry this elephant everywhere; she would place a doll on it and enjoy a wonderful elephant ride. The elephant also has a secret slot to put coins. Next time your child gets some money as a gift she can store it in this elephant. This way your child will learn the habit of saving money from a young age. Moreover it comes in several attractive colours and also types of elephants - the African, the Indian, and the Jumbo. All of them cost the same i.e., ₹ 500. As part of our promotion campaign, we are offering it at ₹ 300 for our first 100 customers." You say, "Wow, you think my child will like this elephant?"

Gradually the salesman observes the customer's body language, gestures and says, "Sir, would you like to hear about the premium and ultra-premium elephants as well?" You say, "Go ahead". The salesman continues, "Sir, this one is called as the budge elephant. It is made of ordinary plastic, all its joints are fixed. It is called the 'rigid elephant'. None of its parts can move. Unlike the other one this does not have a carrier and it comes in a single colour - black. This costs ₹ 200. As I said earlier, the promotion discount is applicable to this too and all you have to pay is ₹ 100."

"Here is the ultra-premium elephant. This is sold under one registered trademark of "Hathi mere Sathi". It comes with a coupon of a free elephant ride in any of the zoos in the city." What is happening is here is that the salesman is engaging the customer in a way that the customer feels that the product is tailored for him. The salesman goes on, "Sir, this comes with a unique colour of white and looks really beautiful. Sir, by any chance have you seen the drawing rooms of the actors Amir Khan or

Salman Khan? You answer, "No". The salesman replies, "No problem Sir. Here is the photograph of the drawing room. The elephant that you see here is the same one you are seeing on the wall of the drawing room. Here is our 'Hathi mere Sathi'." See now the salesman is building a brand image. He is giving proof to the customer and making him believe that by owning this elephant he is getting a premium product. Then he goes further, "Sir, this elephant can talk. It can say 'hello'. Sir please say hello." You say hello and the elephant replies to you in the same tone. "Can you please say tail?" When you say tail, the tail of the elephant starts swinging and when you say stop, the swinging stops. Then the salesman asks you to say 'ear'. When you say this, the ears of the elephant start swinging. When you say stop the swinging stops. The salesman says, "Sir, can you bring your head near the ears and say ear? You can feel the air. That is the uniqueness of the elephant's ear. You can feel cool. Unlike the other elephants, this elephant has all the features like carrier and other things. It also has additional jewels around its head and its neck making it look like the King elephant. It also has a camera and a secret jewel key that can open the carrier under the stomach of the elephant. This will safeguard your child's savings."

Obviously, the customer, after listening to all this will ask the price of the elephant. The salesman says, "Sir, it costs

₹ 1000. However, as a special promotional offer valid for only today you get a discount of Rs.500 on this ultra-premium elephant including the elephant ride in the zoo.

What do you think as customer? Which one would you buy - the ₹ 100 one, the ₹ 200 one or the ₹ 500 one? Many end up choosing the ₹ 500 one, the "Hathi mere Sathi".

Why do you think the customer wants to buy this particular elephant? It is because the salesman has projected the value of the elephant in multiples of 500 in the customer's mind including the emotional value making it priceless. The customer thinks he/she is getting more value than what he/she is paying for. It includes the priceless feeling of owning that elephant which is kept in a celebrity's house. He/she feels it is not an ordinary elephant, not even a premium but an ultra-premium one. It is worth gifting it to the child.

Folks, this is value selling. Only when the product and its features are able to occupy the customer's mind with more value for what he/she is paying, the sale has happened. This is when the value is occurring. The customer never pays for you or your manufacturing cost. The customer always pays for what the product can do to his mind and how he would feel after buying the product. Apart from its basic or main utility, the customer should feel happy and satisfied with buying the product. The value projected by the product is more important than the cost and the salesman has to talk about its various benefits to the customer rather than its cost. Always keep in mind the customer's feeling towards the product when you sell it to him. This will also increase your and your company's value and contribute to boosting the sales and thereby the profits of the company.

CHAPTER 8

ENSURING CUSTOMER SATISFACTION

"Everyone is in the business of Customer Satisfaction. Who are Your Customers and how are they doing?"
– Brian Tracy

After having gone through various attributes that drive sales, that make sales happen, we come to the most important aspect, the epicentre of the entire business — Customer Satisfaction. Let us first understand what customer satisfaction is. Let us take a simple example of brushing our teeth. This requires basic things like toothpaste and toothbrush. Now say you are travelling on a train. You have had a good night's sleep in the A/C coach and wake up refreshed. Now you want to brush your teeth. But when you open the suitcase you realize the bristles on the brush are completely bent as it was pressed down by weight of the other things in your bag. You brush but are not satisfied with the experience. You will not get the same feeling of brushing with a brush with straight bristles. The experience is not the same. Observe your feelings now. This would not have happened if you had packed the brush in a box. Now say your brush is fine but the toothpaste you have brought along is leaking. Somehow you push the tube, take the paste and brush. As you finish brushing your teeth, you open the tap and find to your dismay that there is no water. Once again observe the feeling. We will come back to this.

There is no water in the tap and you get an idea of using the mineral water bottle that you had purchased the previous night and somehow you complete the job of brushing your teeth.

Ask yourself the following questions:

a) What were your expectations from the brush?

b) What were your expectations from the tube of paste?

c) What were your expectations from the basin tap?

Now imagine you owned a famous brand that manufactures toothpaste and toothbrush. How would you design your product? How would you make sure that the user's experience is delightful? How would you differentiate your product and the experience and feeling associated with it?

You are on both sides-the user and the manufacturer. I am sure you are discovering the disconnect.

Keeping all these feelings, emotions and thoughts and your overall experience in mind, rate the customer satisfaction that you would give to the company that had made the brush and paste.

Folks that is customer satisfaction for you. Let us take the same situation but another example. Say a shaving kit. You are carrying the Gillette's latest product. It has multiple blades, has a layer of gel for smooth shaving and doesn't have sharp exposed edges that prick you. This is unlike the old kit where you have to assemble the blade in the shaving kit. You get a smooth shave with this Gillette kit and a lovely experience. You didn't have to struggle to open the handbag and demonstrating to the airport security that the kit is intended only for shaving and explain your intentions.

In this case, sit back and repeat the exercise of customer satisfaction that we did with the toothpaste and toothbrush. 1 being poor and 10 being the best, rate your experience. You start wondering if there is anything that is beyond 10 for you to rate.

This brings us to the topic of looking beyond the horizon of customer satisfaction that is customer delight. You mark 10 and put a smiley next to it. Now this is delivering value to the customer that is beyond expectation. Yes, it is the delight that matters. In other words, customer satisfaction is how well the product meets the expectation of the customer. Further, it is not just the product but the overall experience of the customer i.e., how it impacts his emotions, feelings etc.

This satisfaction level is what defines how much the customer is willing to pay, reward the company back by paying an extra-premium compared to other brands prices. Thus customer satisfaction is an important parameter that redefines whether the sales will repeat or will it be a onetime affair? Will it be at the cost price or at a cost that is packaged with premium or will you land with stocks that the customer is not willing to pay for this product anymore? Customer satisfaction is not just the product functionality but it is a combination of many aspects. A typical example is of one when the customer understands the salesman when he came to buy the product, his overall experience, usage experience, after sales service, availability of spare parts and so on. An ideal attempt would be to give the customer a delightful experience through all the stages of sale and after the sale so that the customer falls in love with the product, brand, and company.

Few of the companies that have attempted and have been quite successful on this path are:

Apple, Amazon, Nike, Gillette, Hewlett Packard, Sony etc.

These companies ensure that the top management read customer emails regularly. They also take care of their employees which has a direct effect on the customer. They build products based on customer desires rather than their development team's opinion. Some of these practices have worked for the companies to be rated on top of most lists in customer satisfaction worldwide.

Customer satisfaction is the parameter that helps one manage and improve business and is an indication of how the customers will treat the company next time. Will they come back or not? Will they recommend the product or service to their family and friends? Will they build the reputation of the company through their word of mouth? It is also important because it helps retain old customers and bring in new ones. Once the levels of satisfaction are high we can be assured that the customers are here to stay with us a long time.

So Folks, in this book I have tried to take you through the process of sale and the various stages of sale and after sales. The customer is the king. He has to be given utmost importance if we have to see our sales grow and business flourish and retain our spot in the market.

Now that you have a better idea about how to go about your sales, retain your customers and employees create a brand that will stand the test of time, it will be much simpler for you to sell a product based on its value. Whenever you make a sale think in terms of the long- term benefits and not the short-term ones. The short- term benefits may look good now but in terms of building your business and retaining your place in the market, you need to have long-term goals.

Sale, give the customer a delightful experience and build a long-term relationship that is sustainable and beneficial to both parties.

Day 1

Day 2

Day 3

Day 4

Day 5

Day 6

Day 7

Day 8

Day 9

Day 10

Day 11

Day 12

Day 13

Day 14

Day 15

Notes

Notes

www.ingramcontent.com/pod-product-compliance
Lightning Source LLC
Chambersburg PA
CBHW030913180526
45163CB00004B/1819